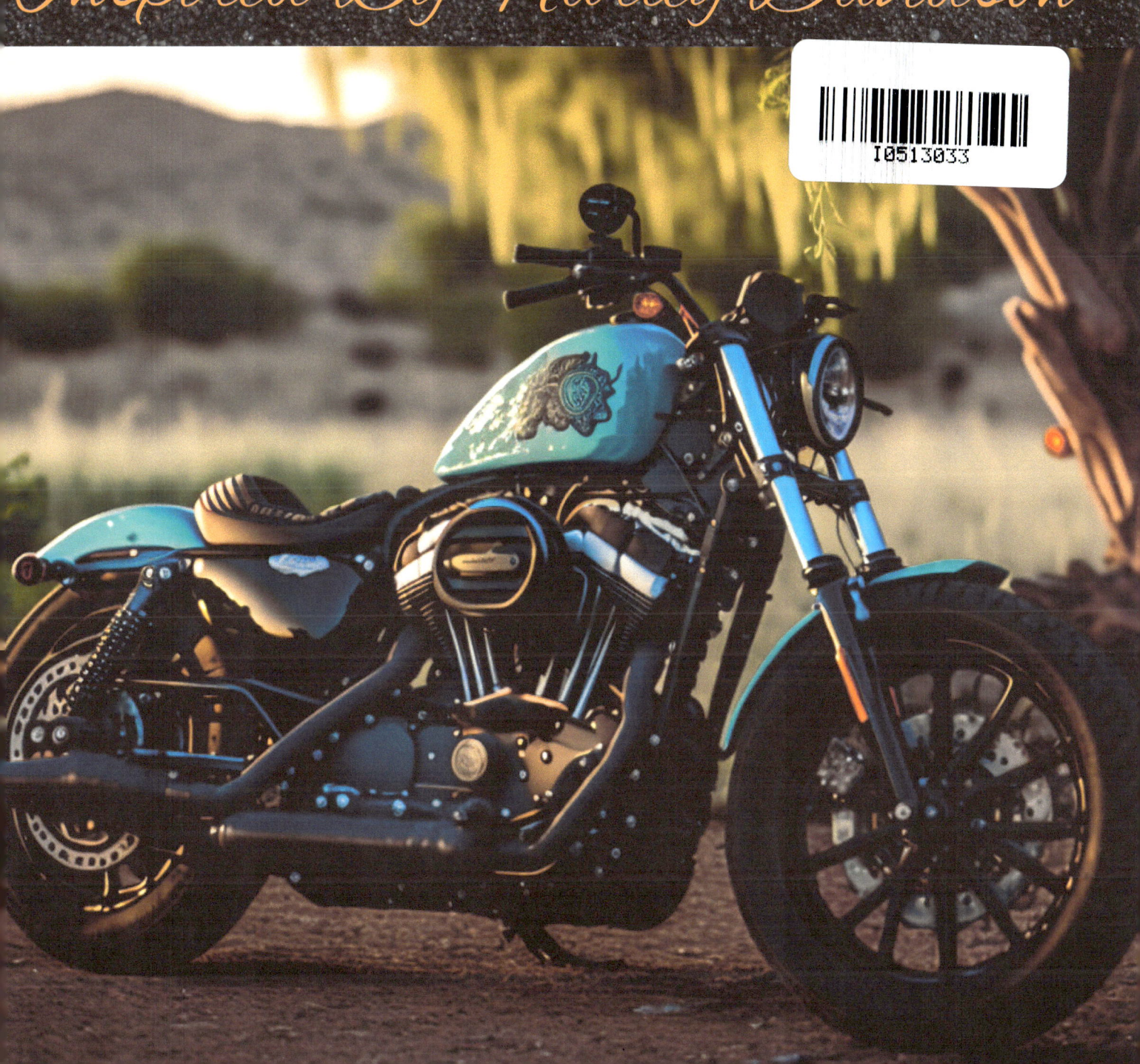

Prompt

A Harley-Davidson Fat Bob motorcycle Luxury awesome classic amazing spectacular Sony Alpha A7 III Canon EF 85mm f/1.2L II USM twilight 8k --ar 16:9

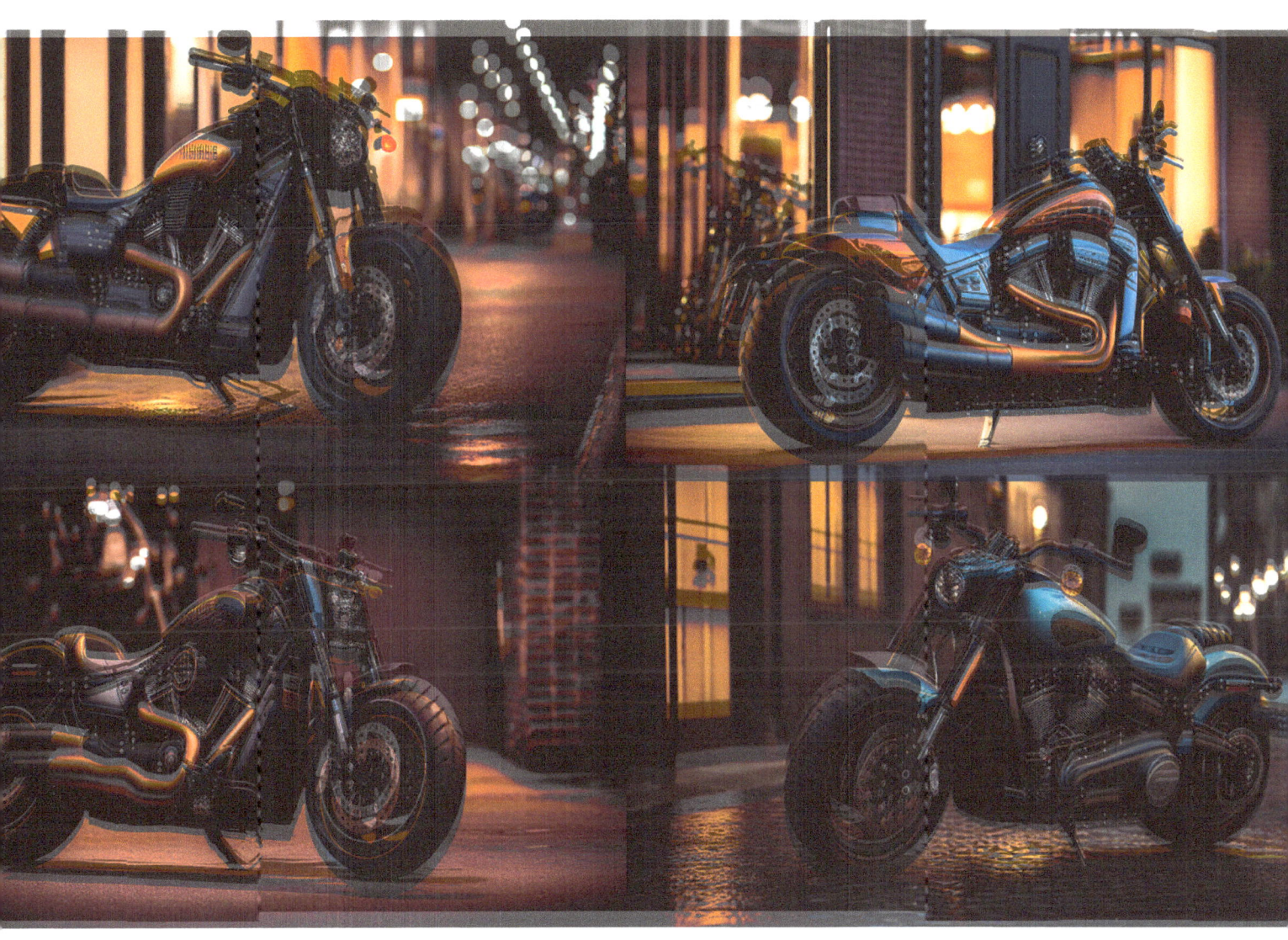

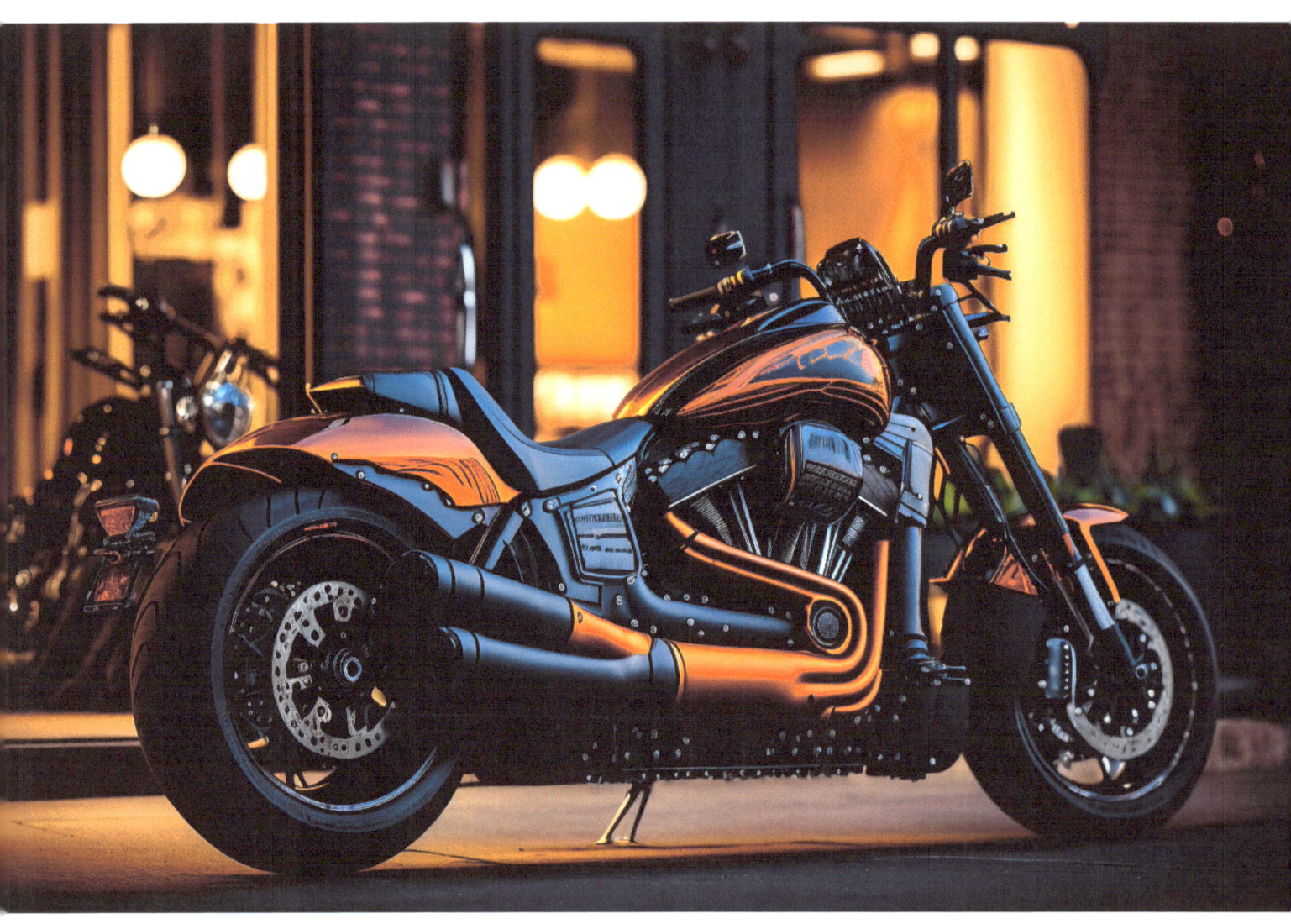

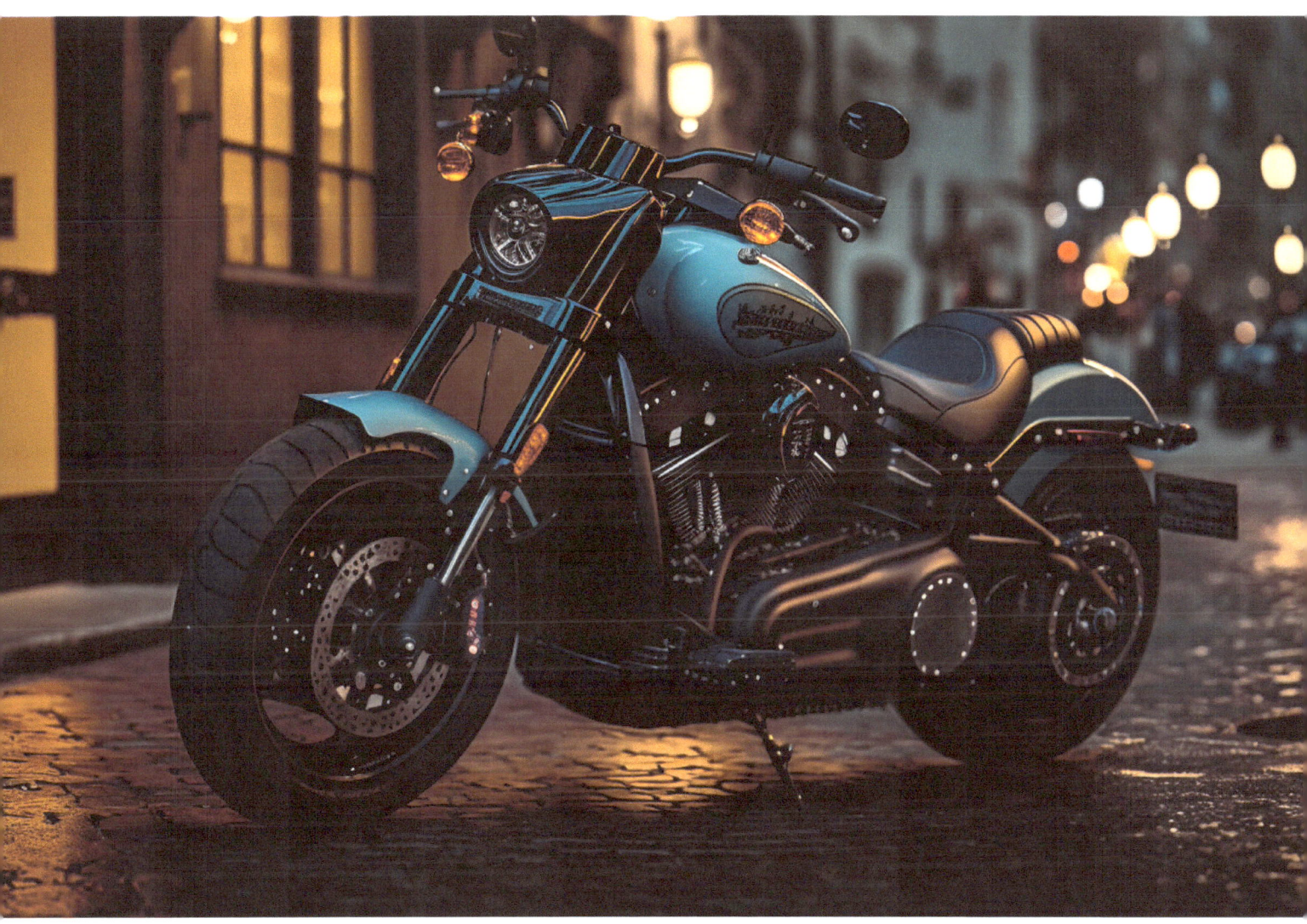

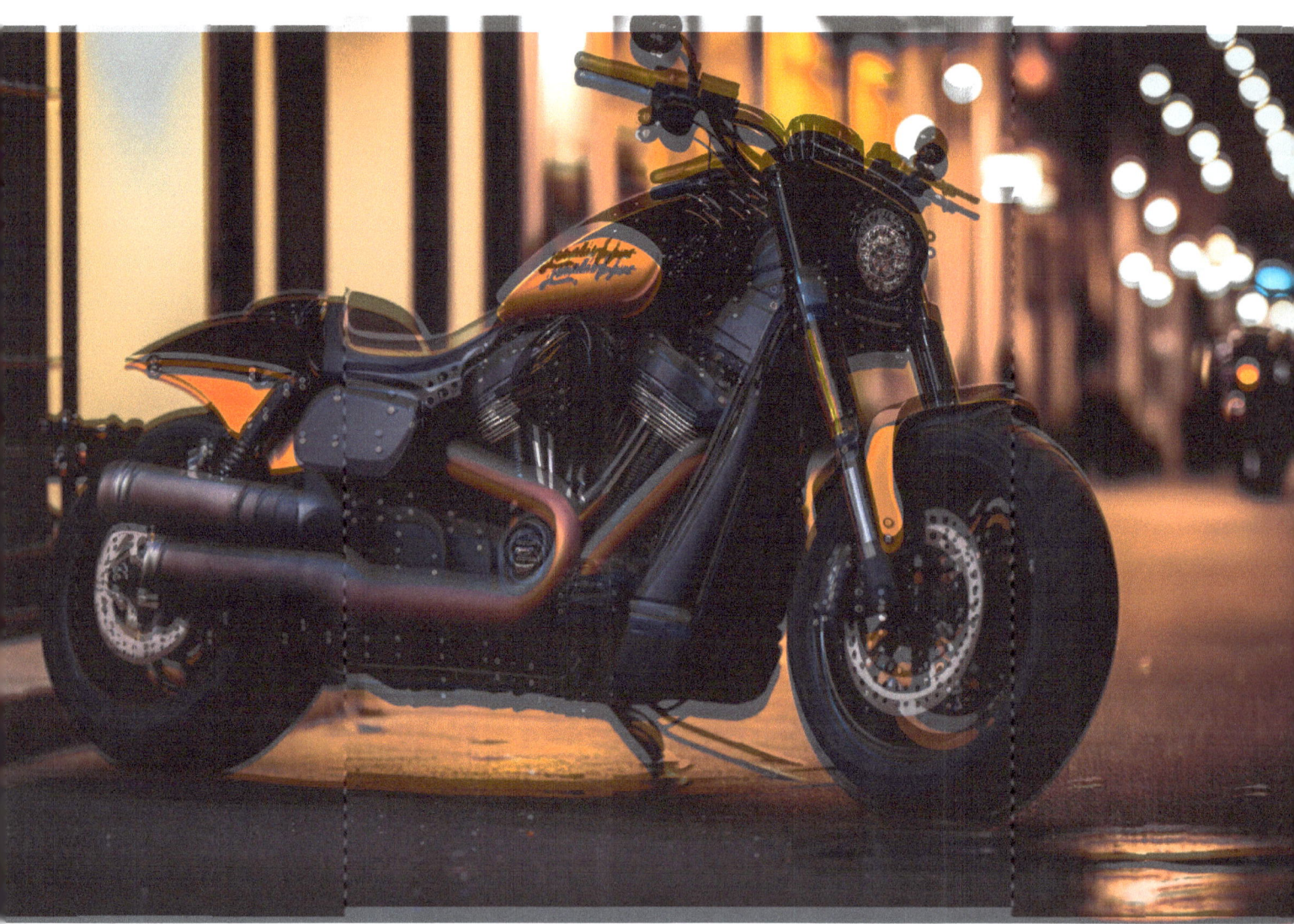

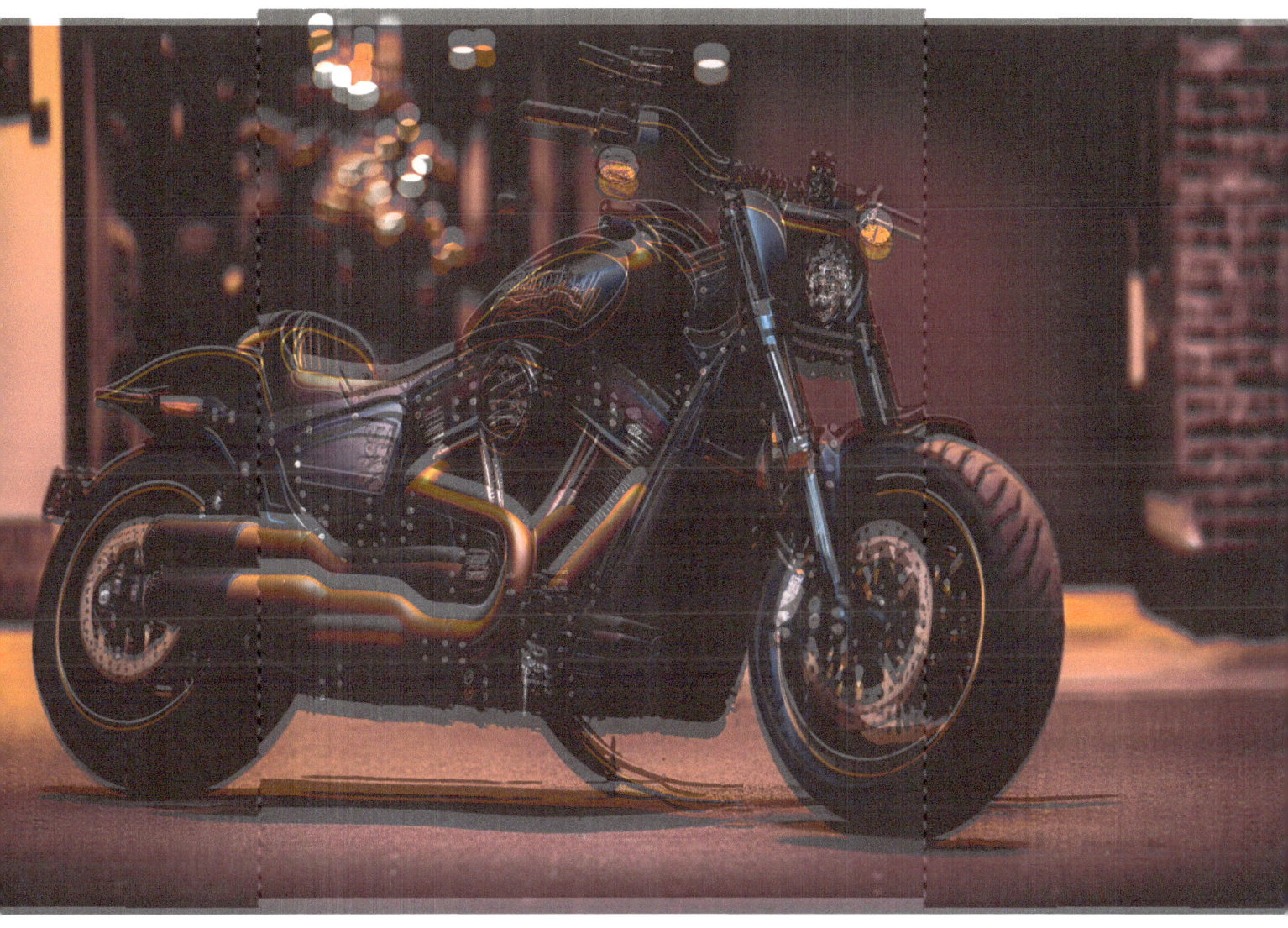

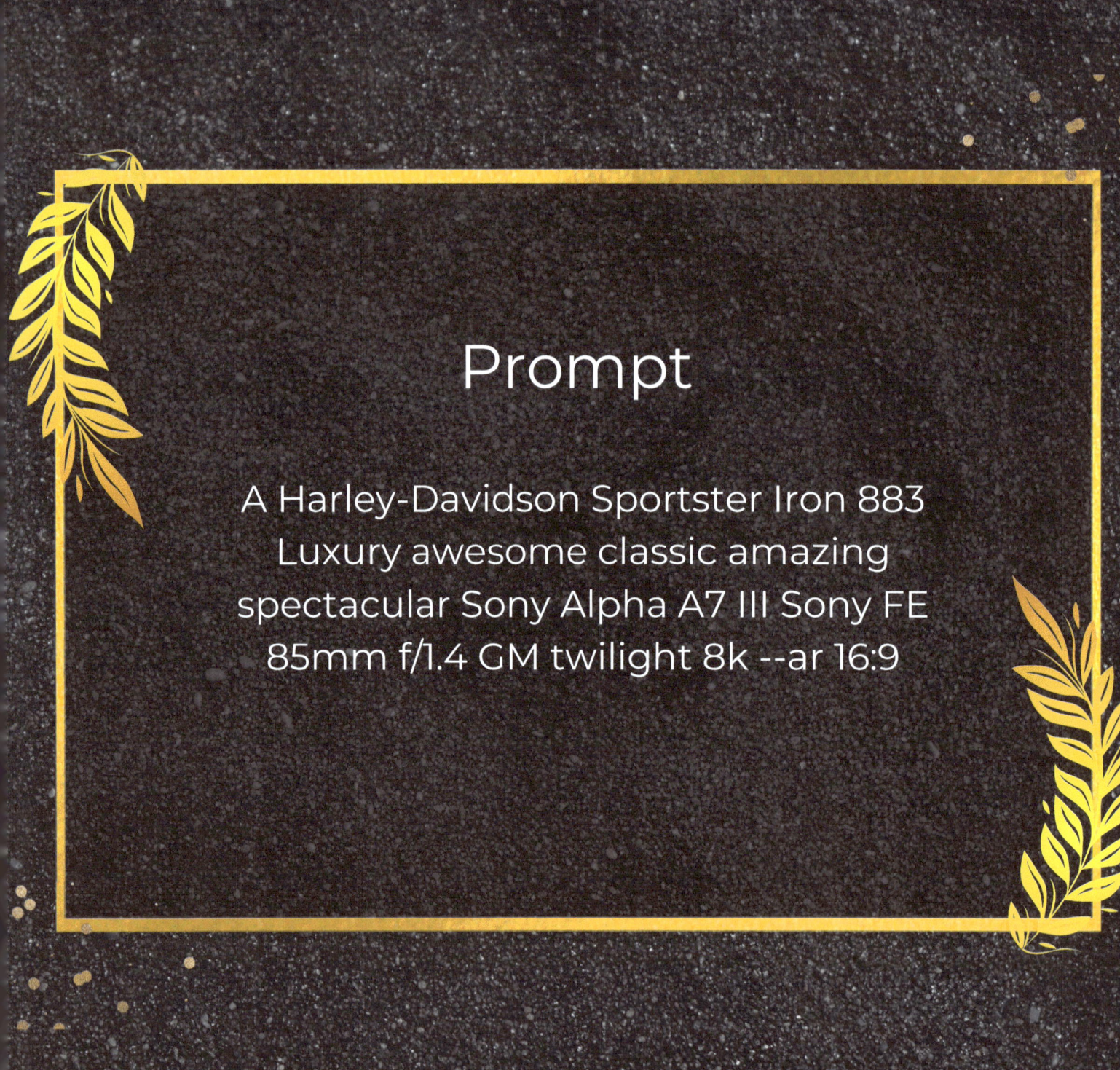

Prompt

A Harley-Davidson Sportster Iron 883 Luxury awesome classic amazing spectacular Sony Alpha A7 III Sony FE 85mm f/1.4 GM twilight 8k --ar 16:9

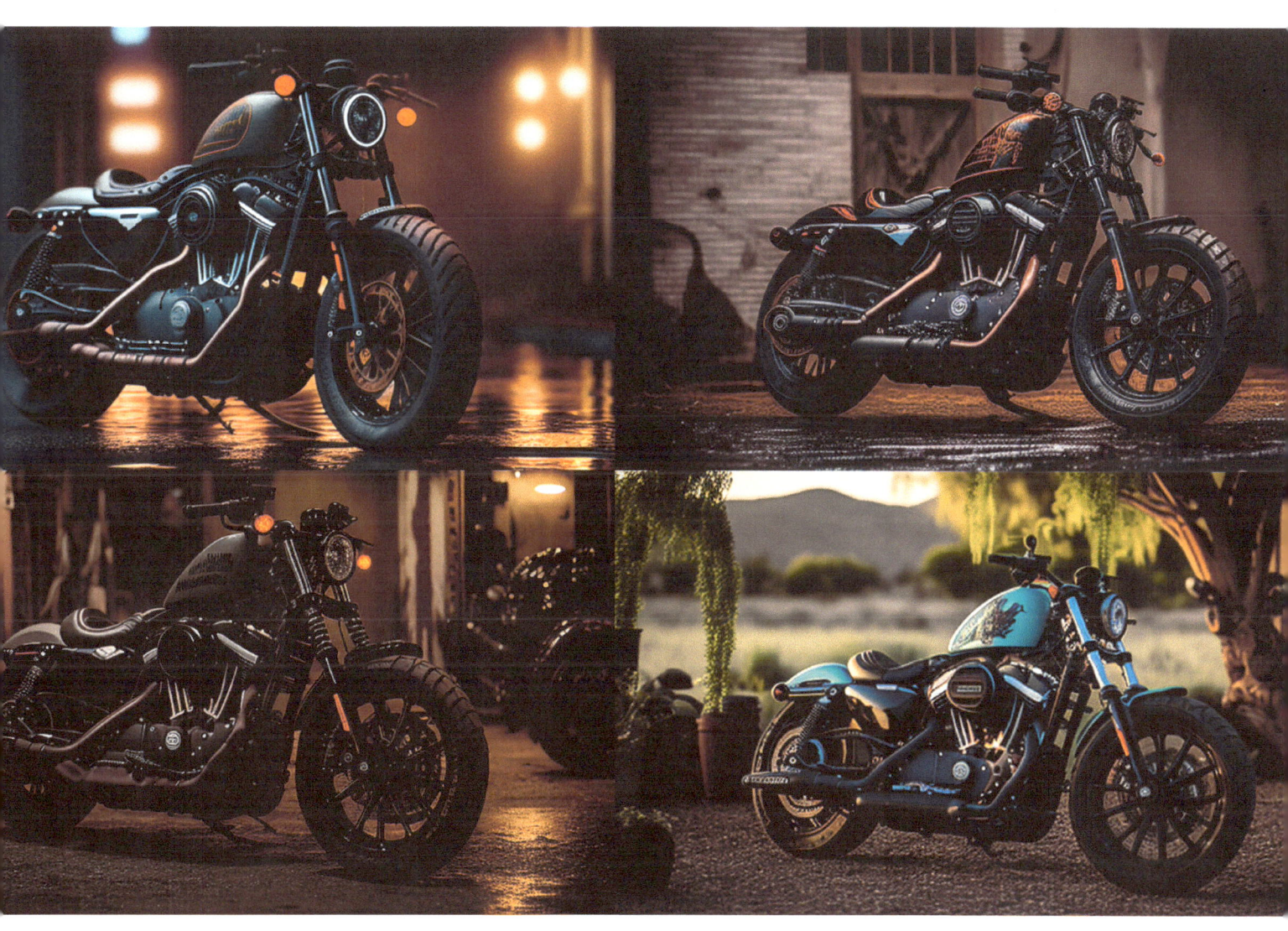

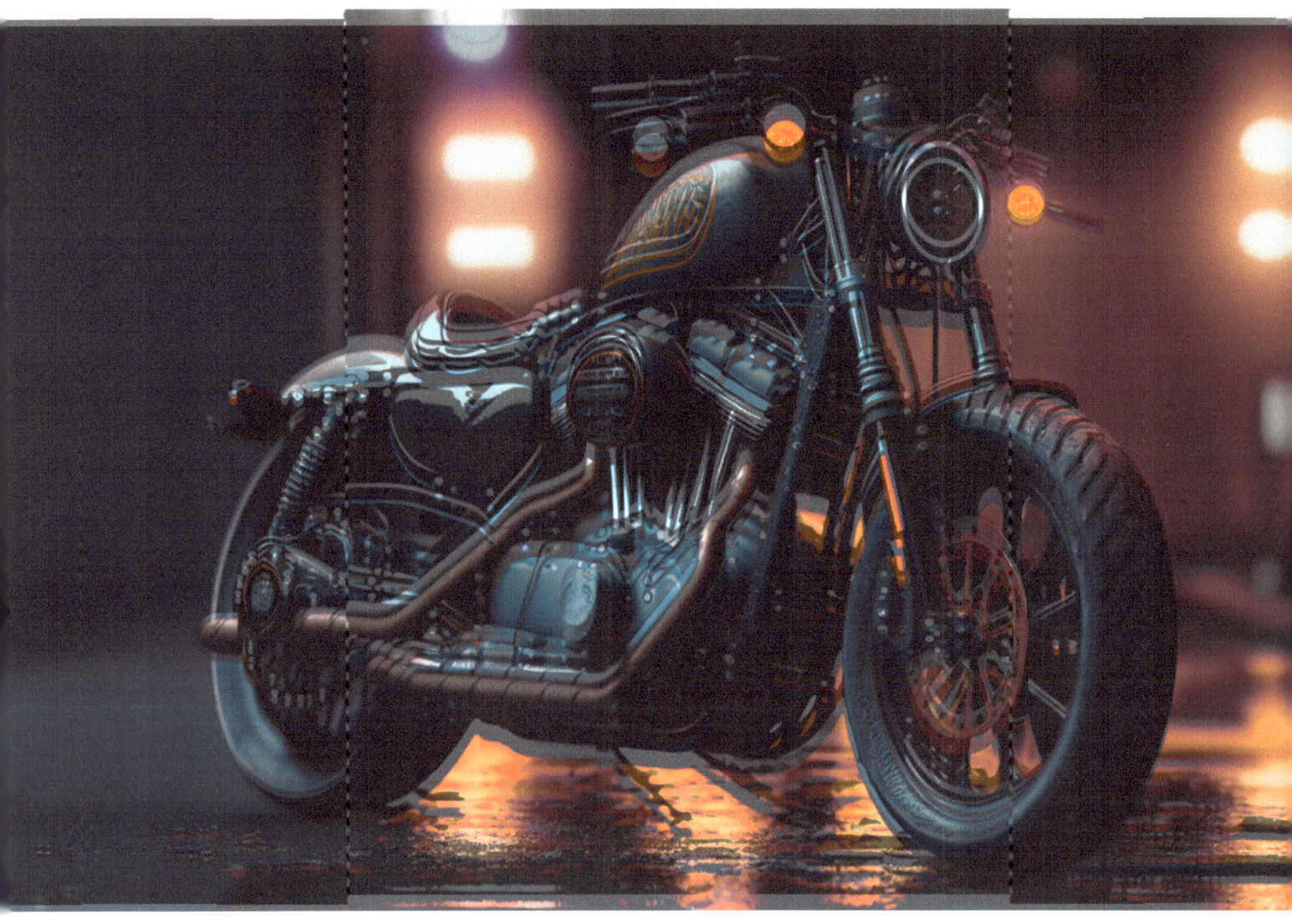

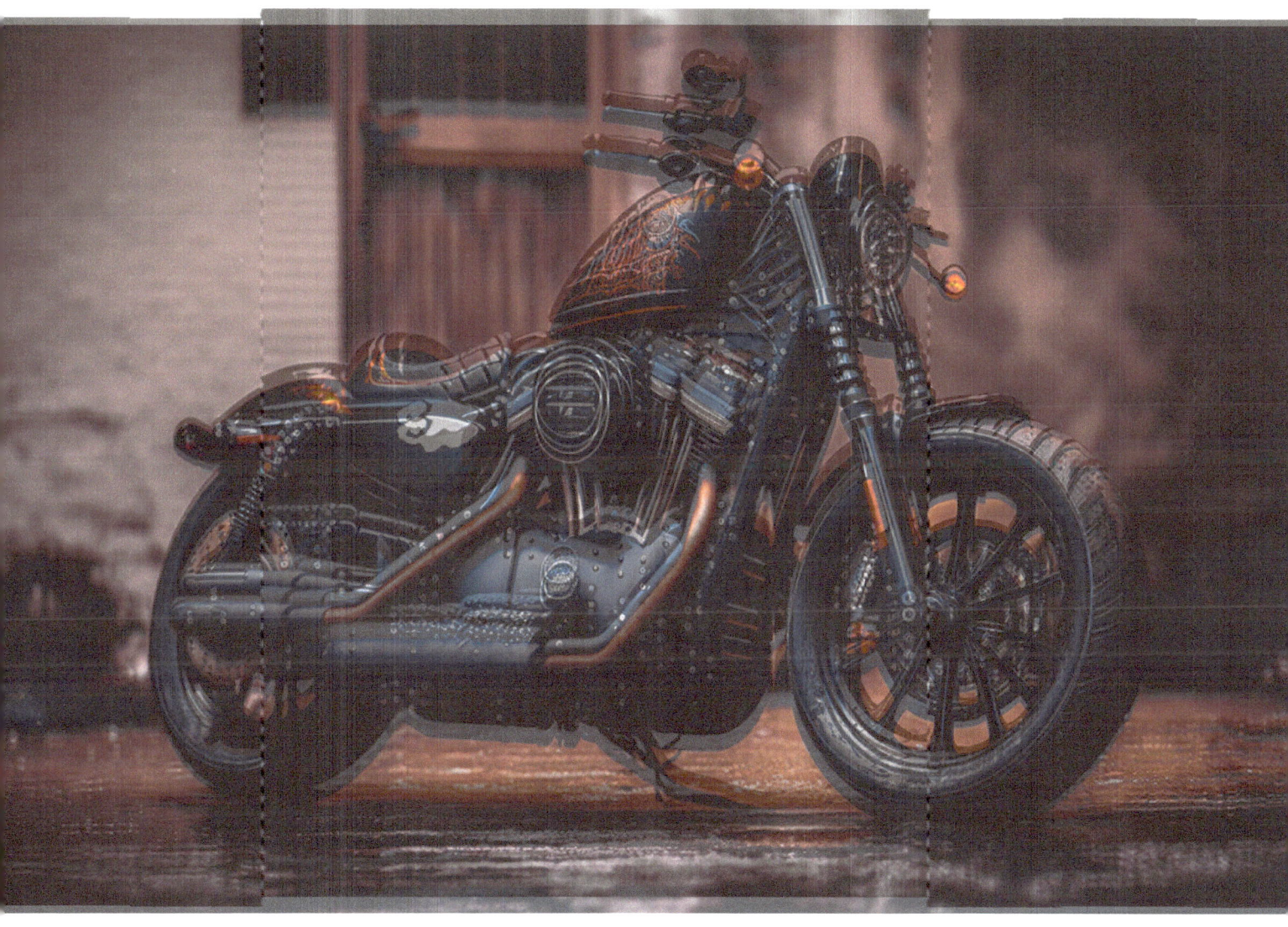

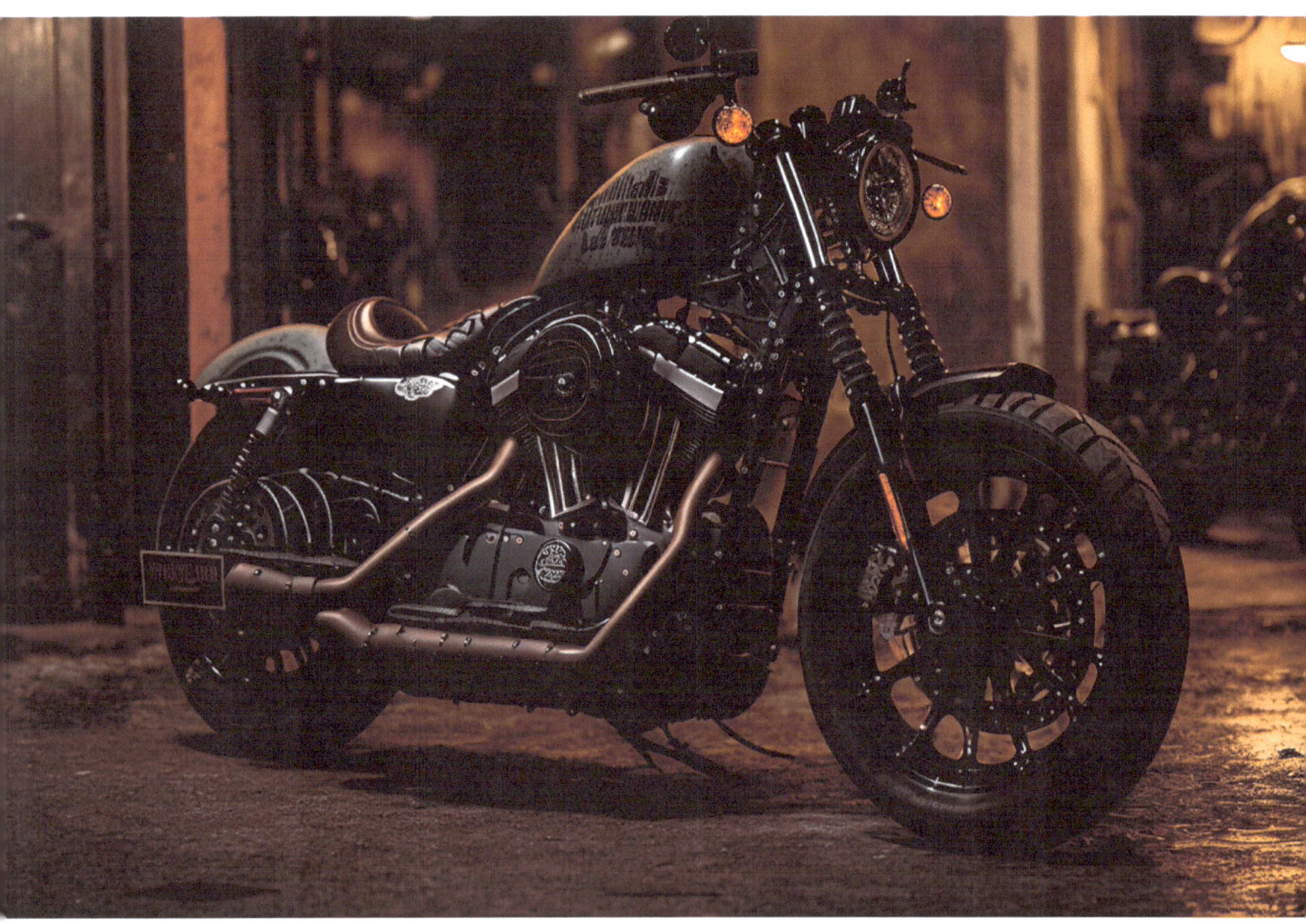

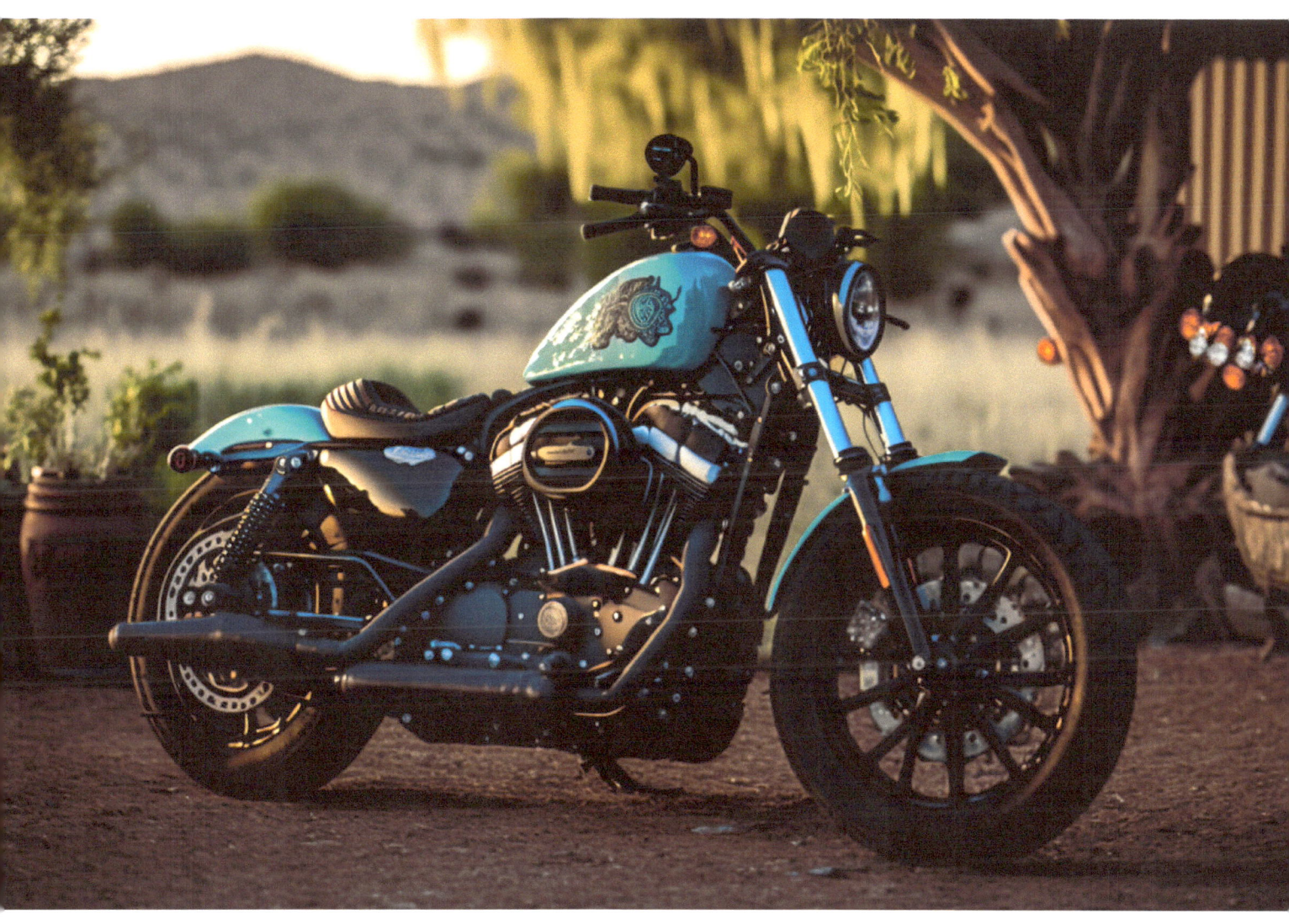

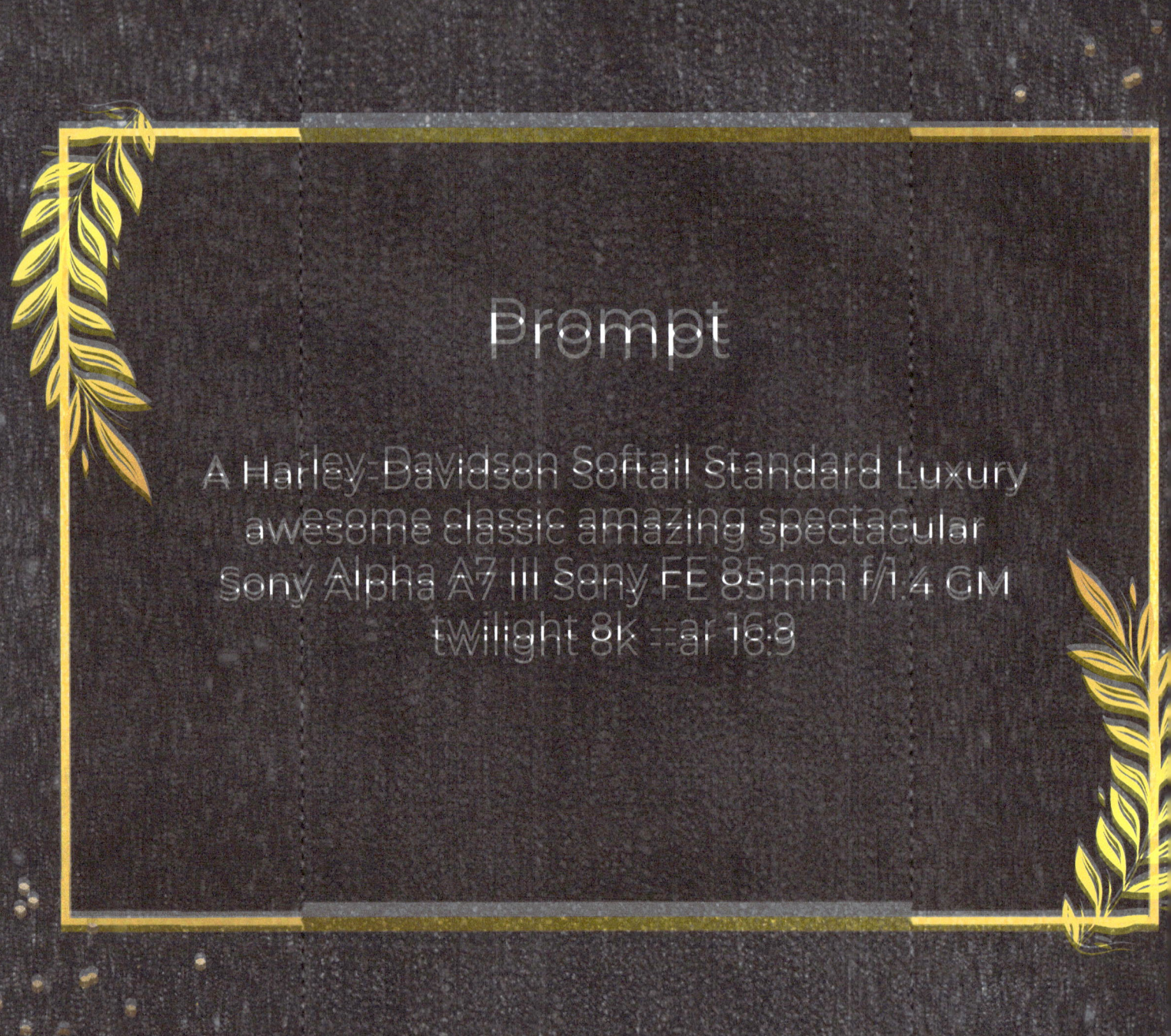

Prompt

A Harley-Davidson Softail Standard Luxury awesome classic amazing spectacular Sony Alpha A7 III Sony FE 85mm f/1.4 GM twilight 8k --ar 16:9

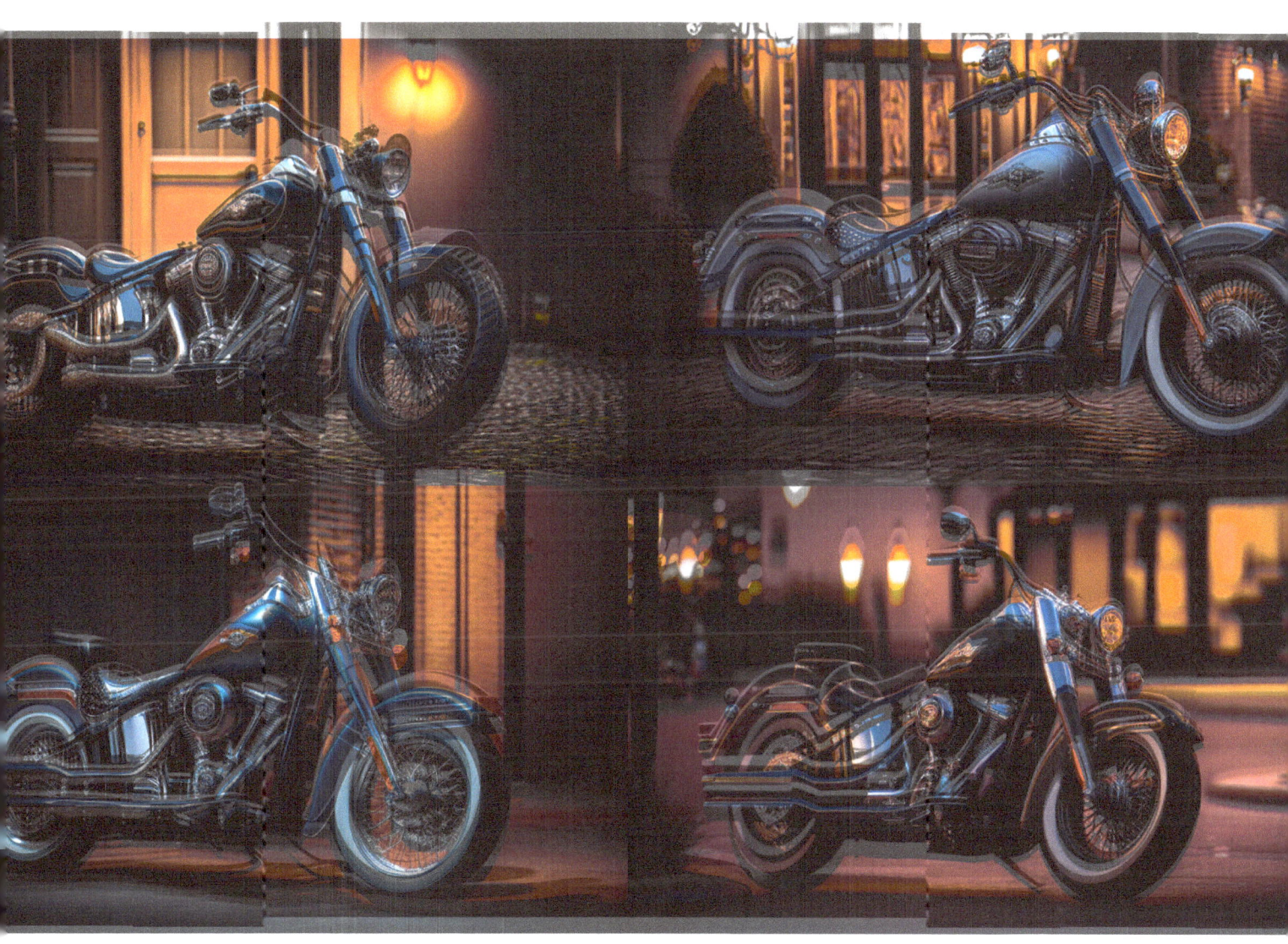

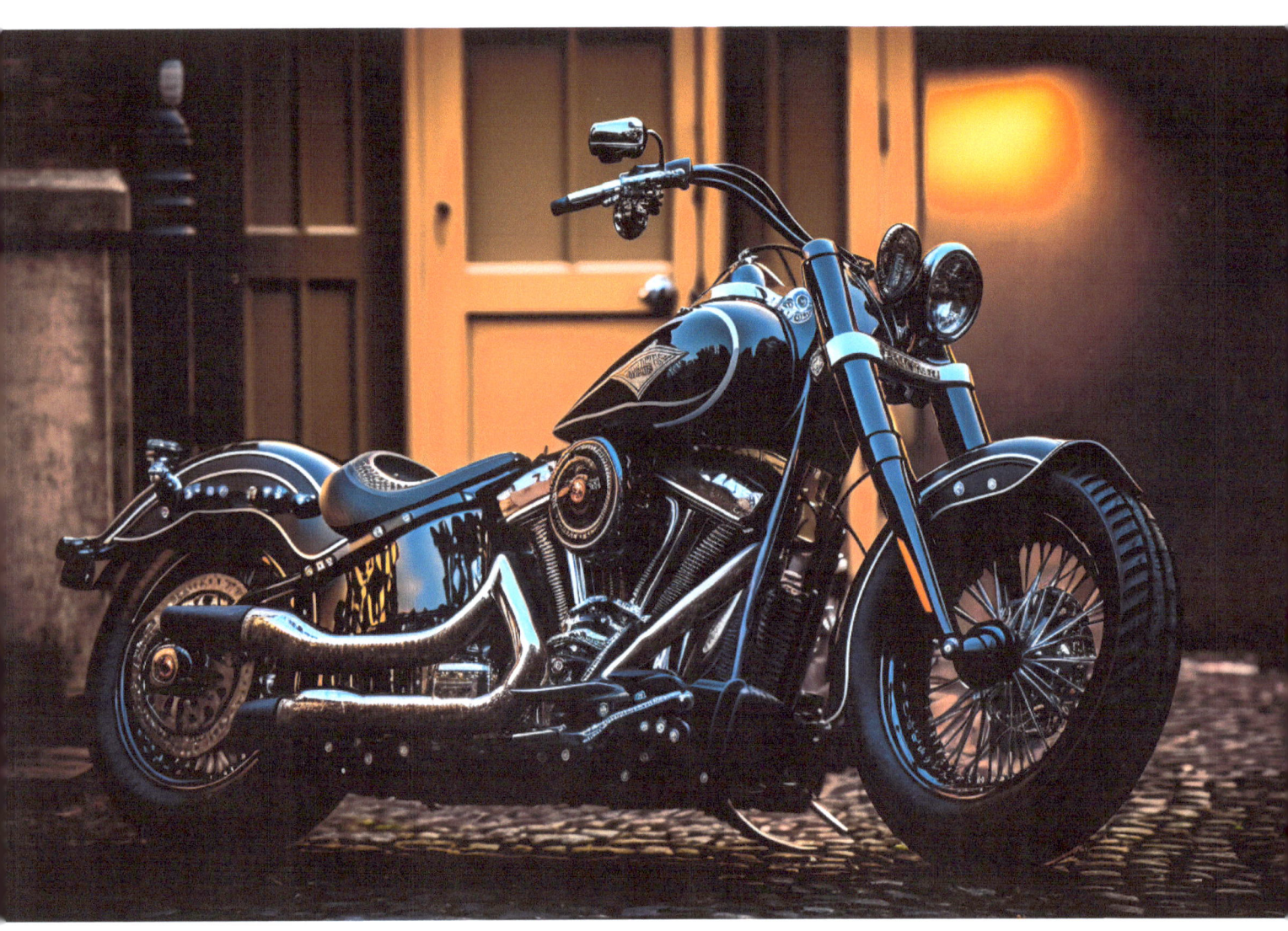

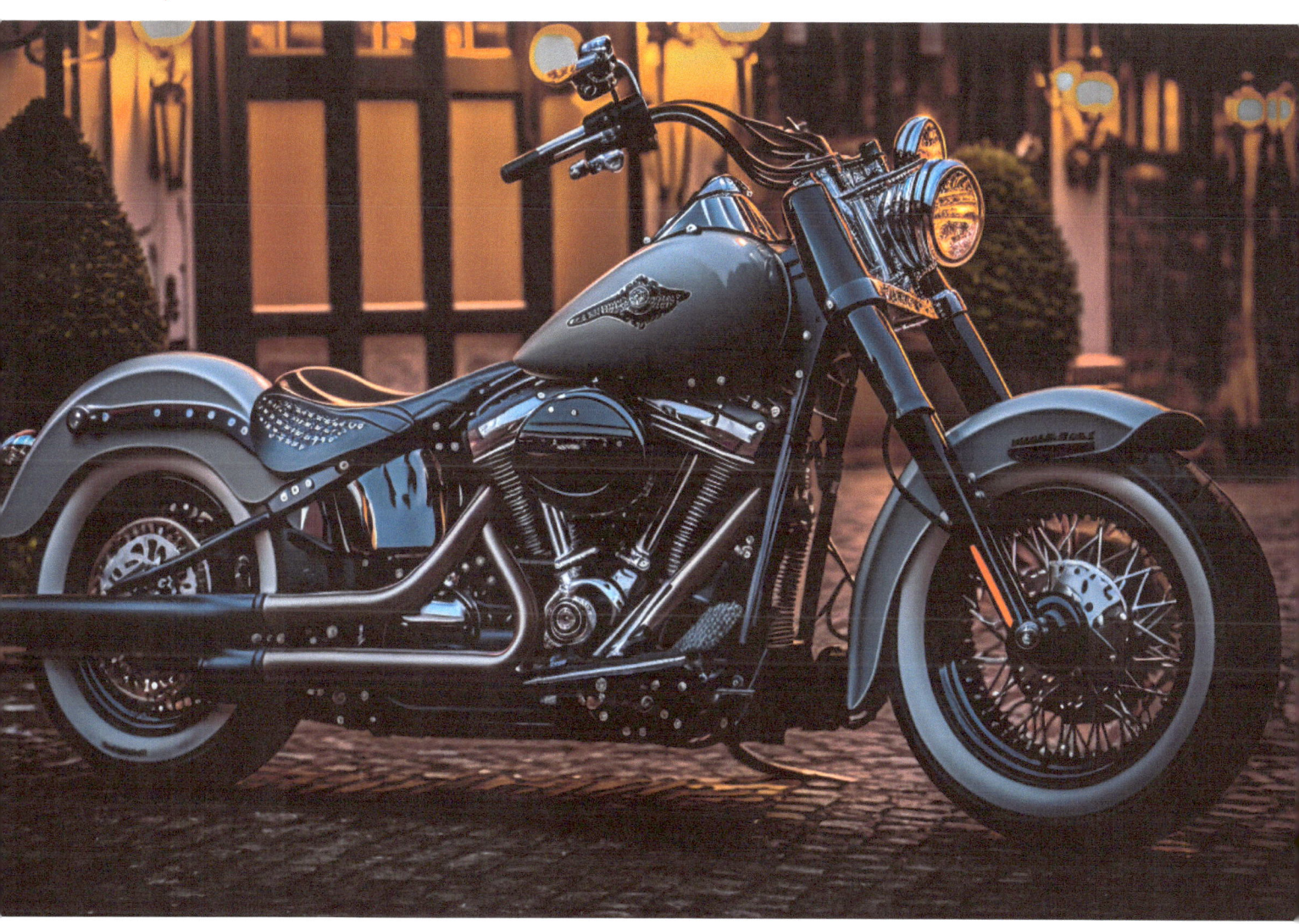

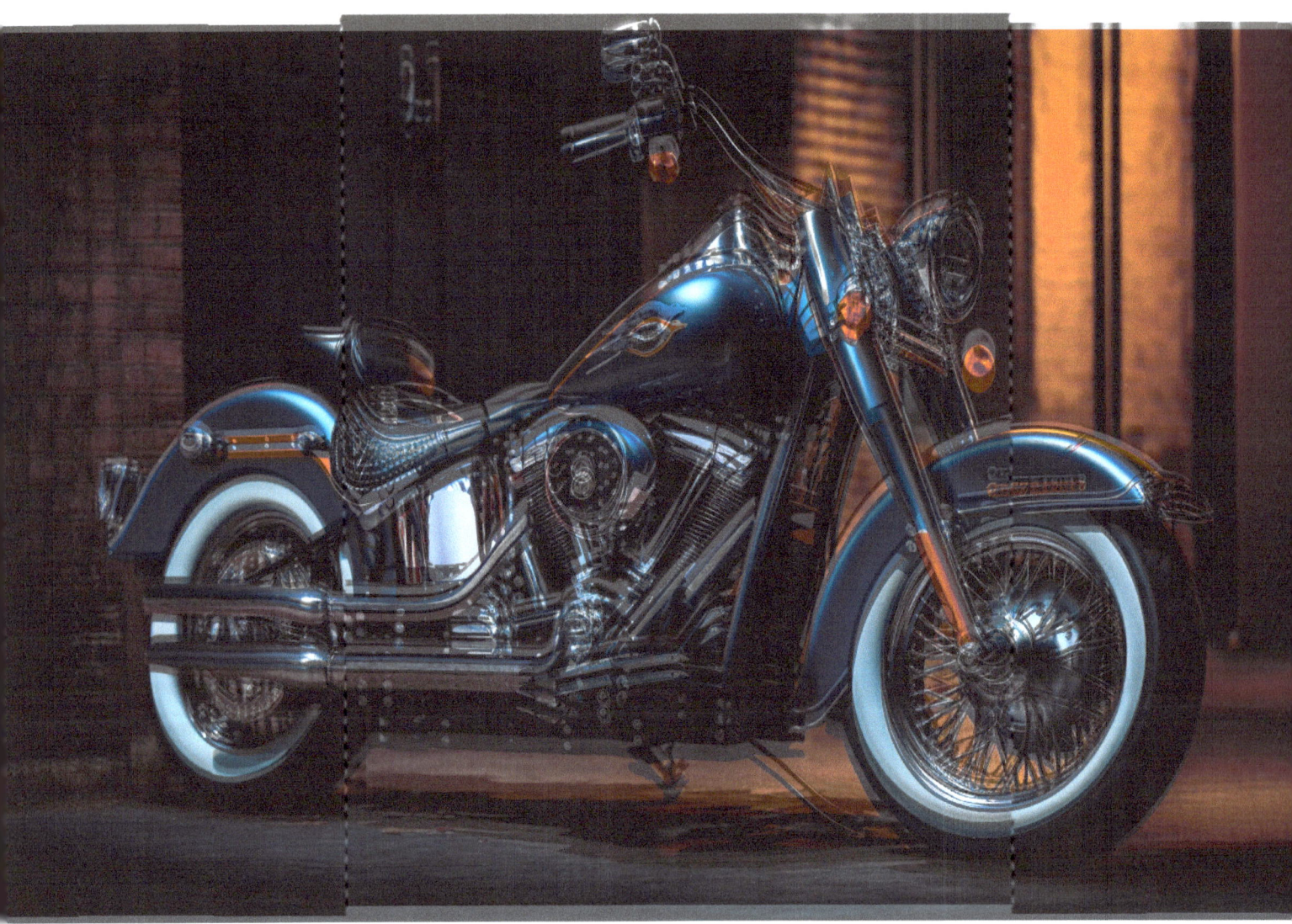

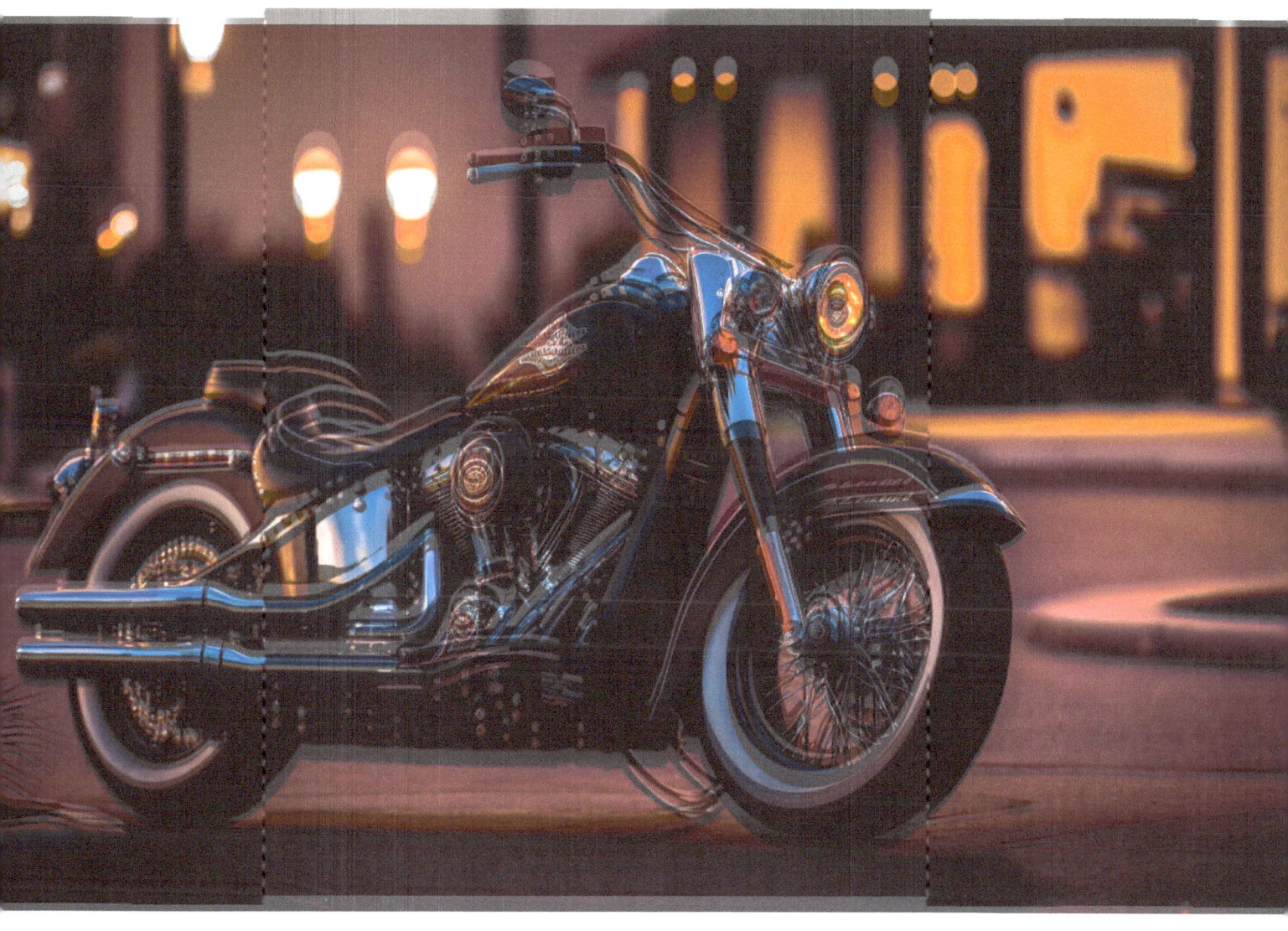

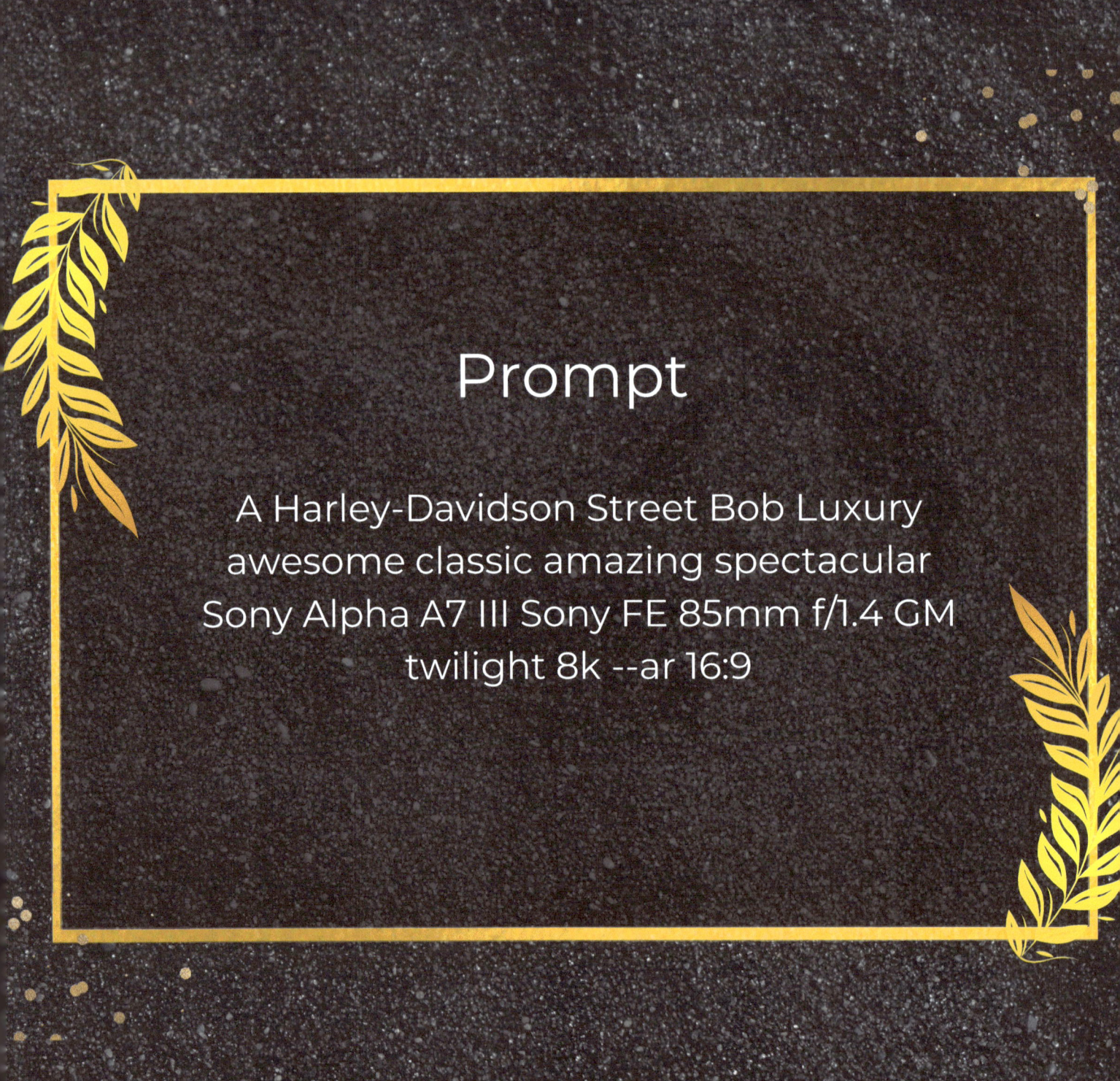

Prompt

A Harley-Davidson Street Bob Luxury awesome classic amazing spectacular Sony Alpha A7 III Sony FE 85mm f/1.4 GM twilight 8k --ar 16:9

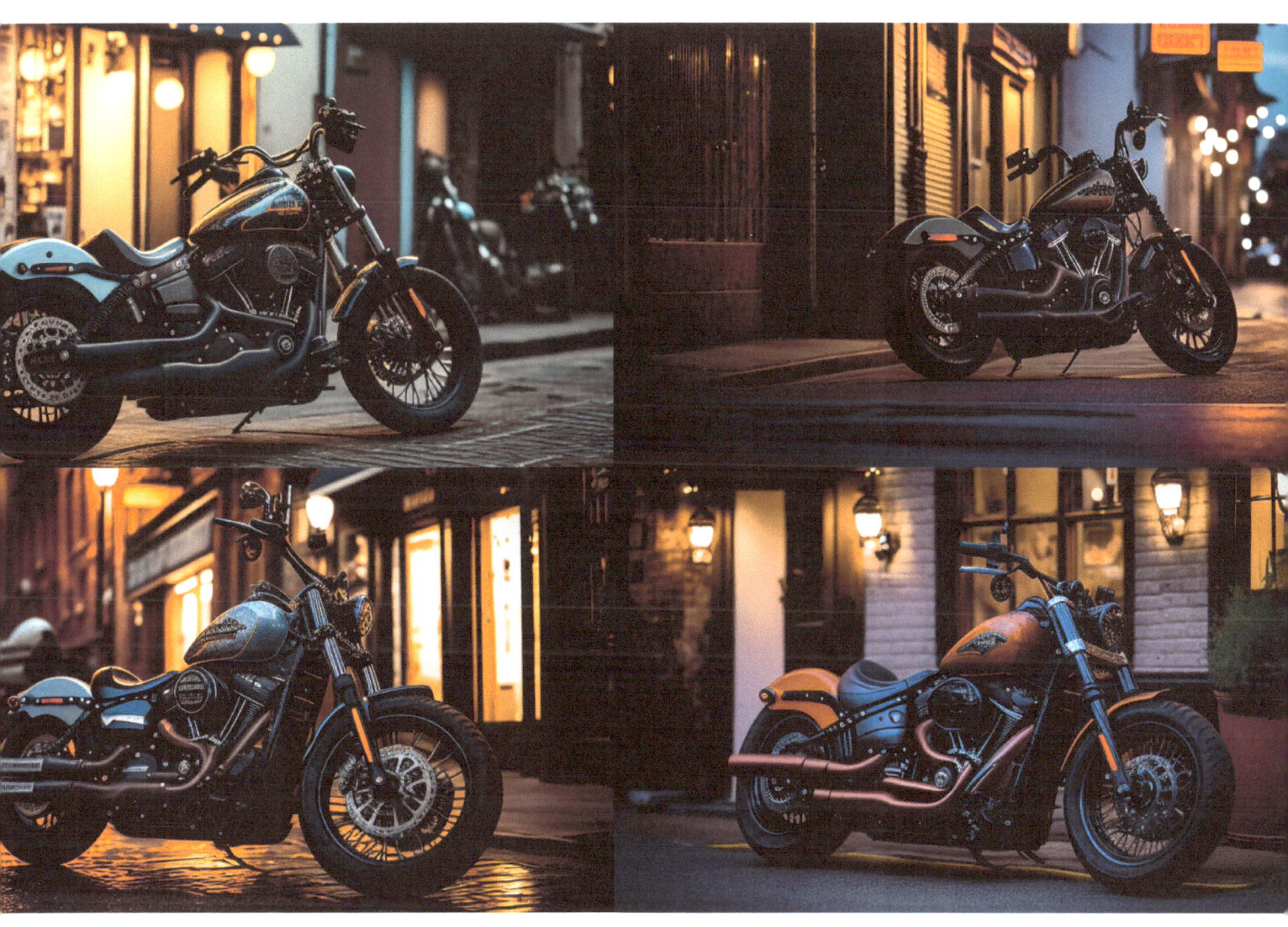

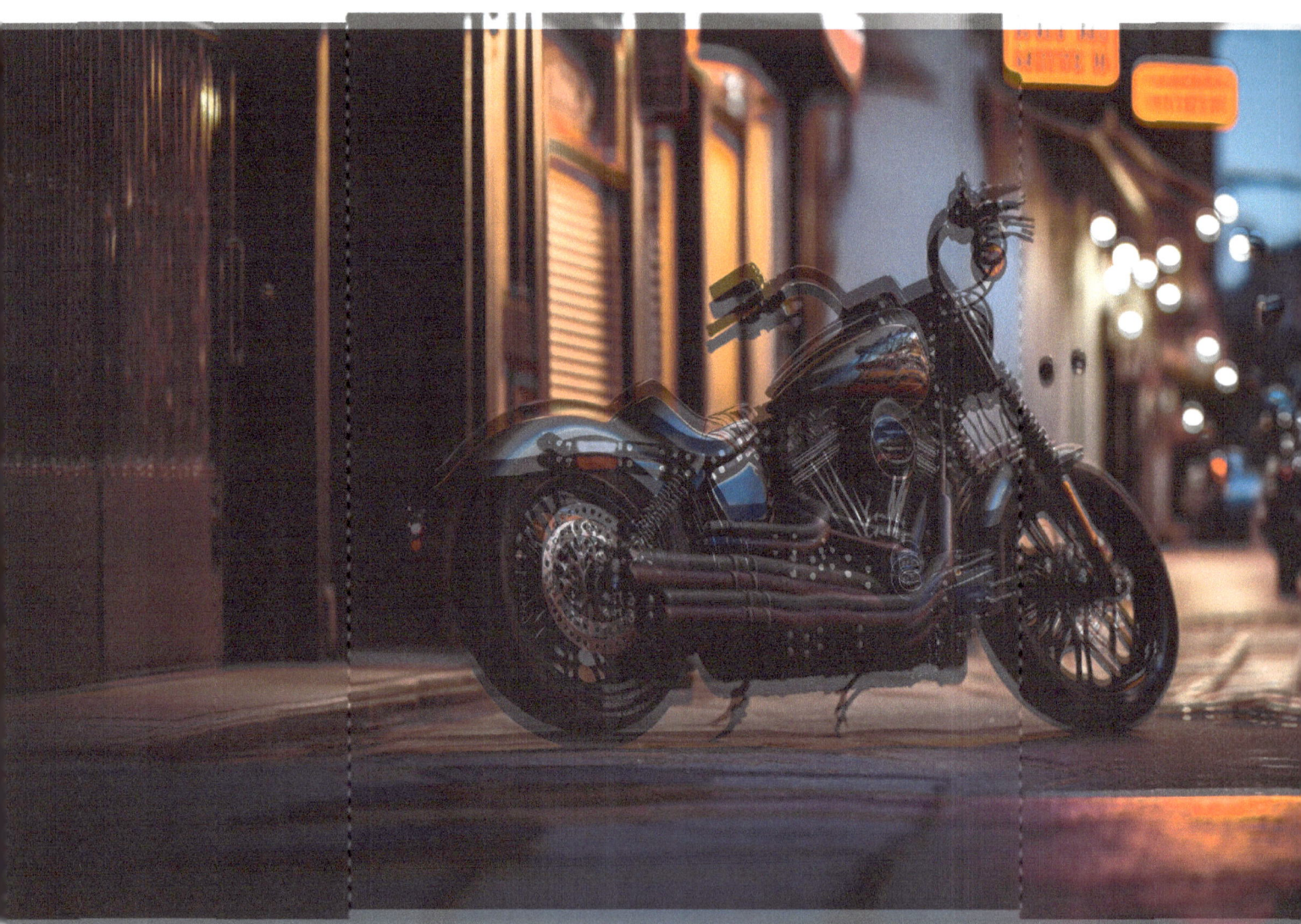

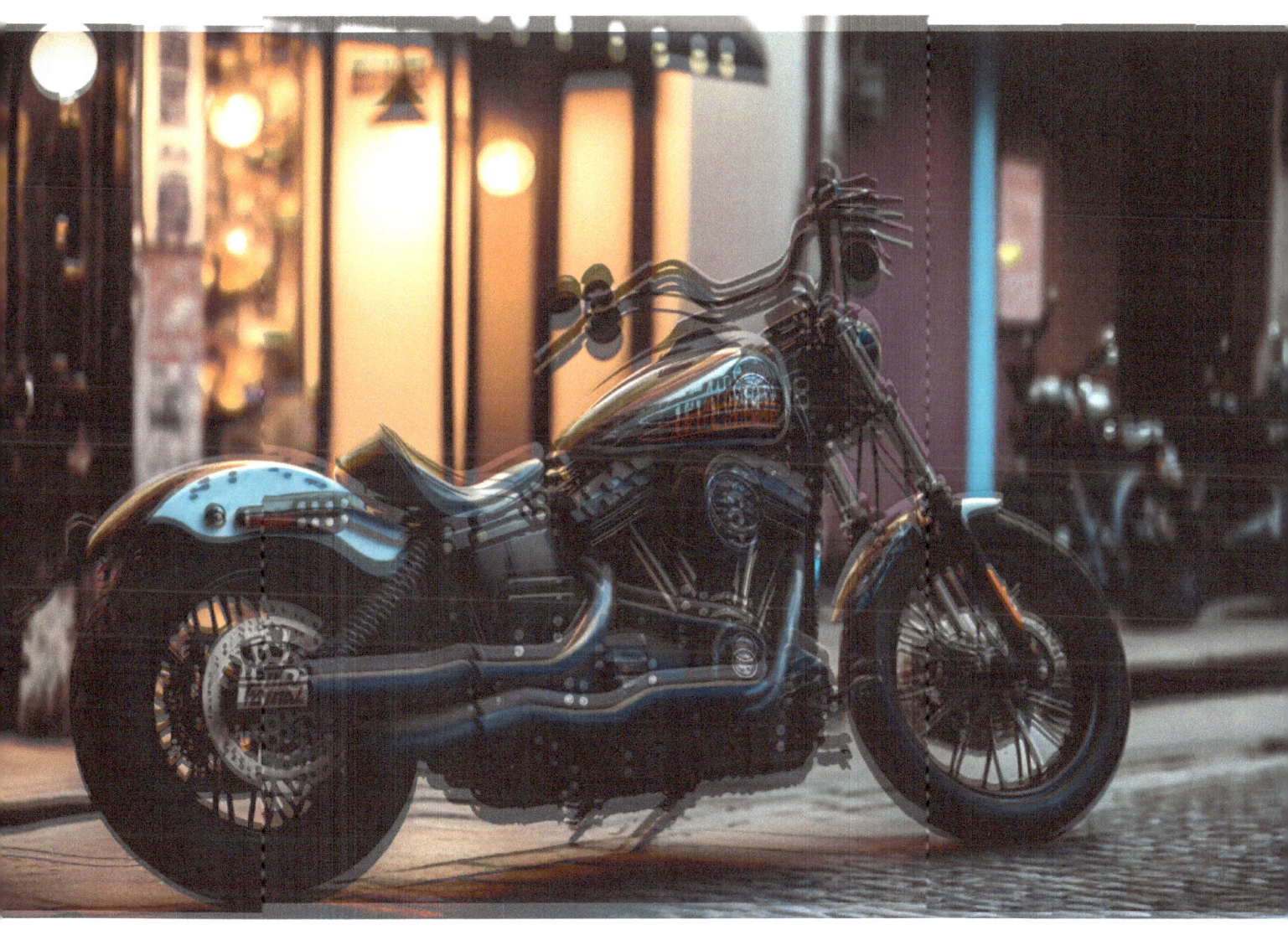

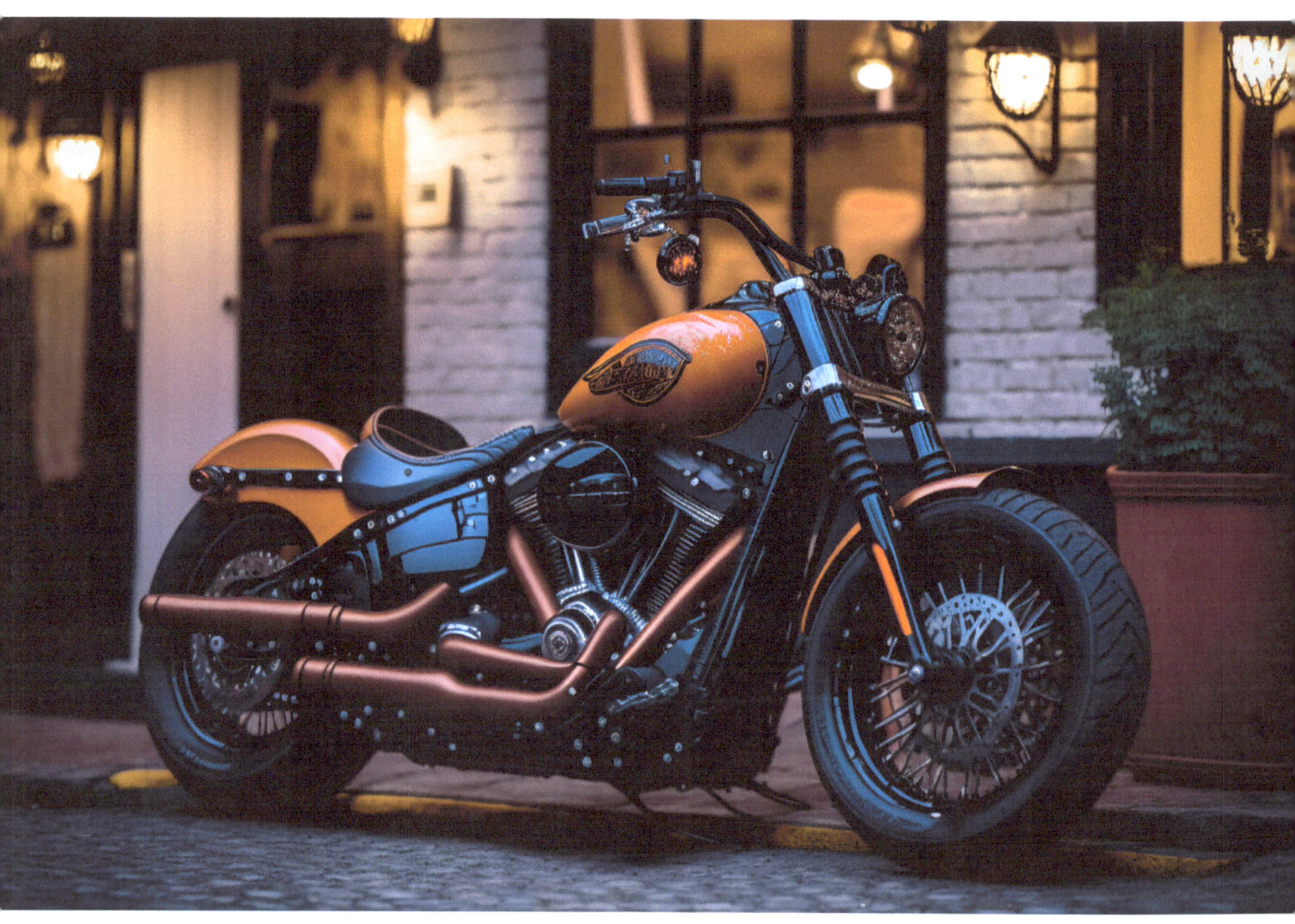

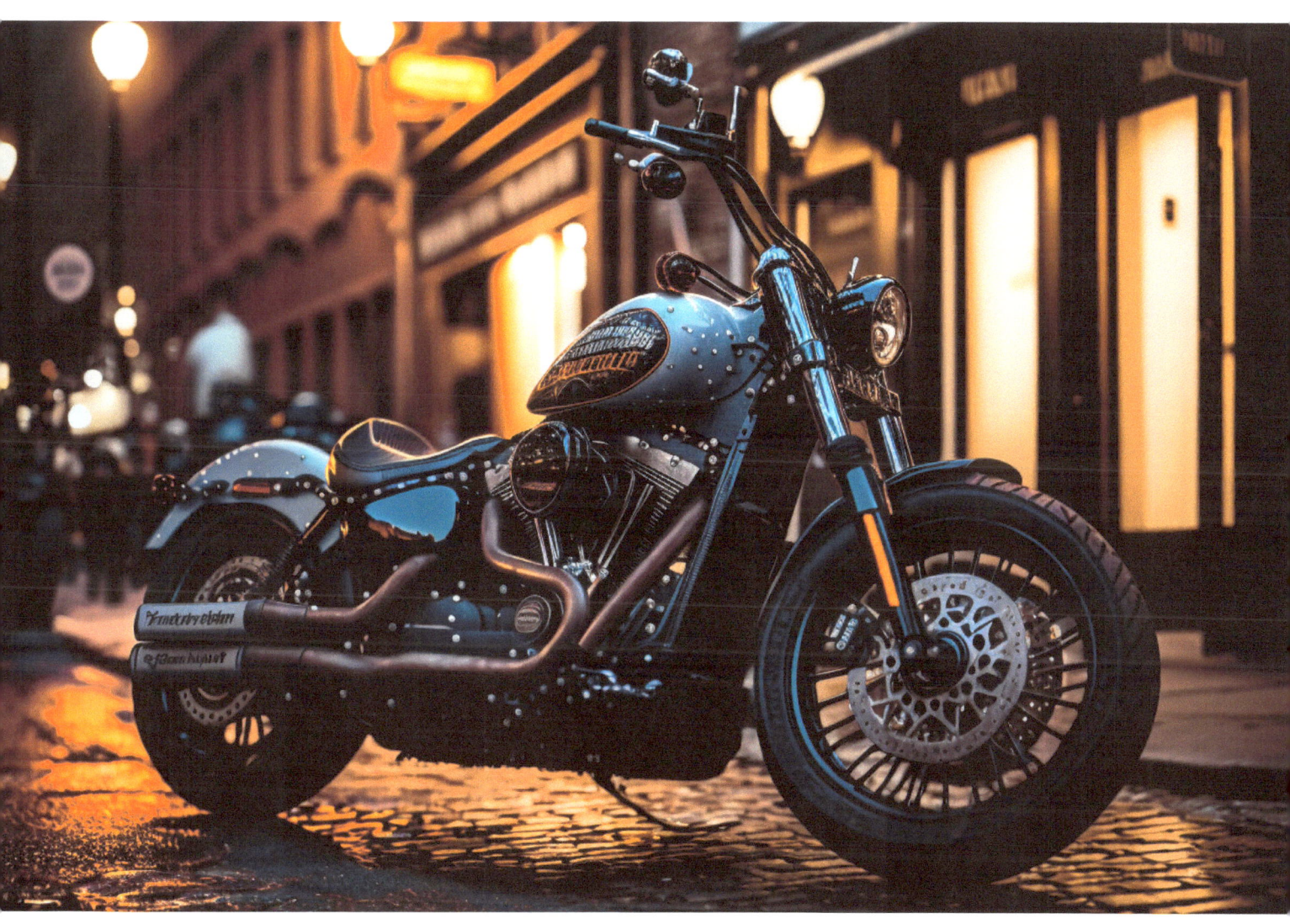

Prompt

A Harley-Davidson Road King Luxury awesome classic amazing spectacular Sony Alpha A7 III Sony FE 85mm f/1.4 GM twilight 8k --ar 16:9

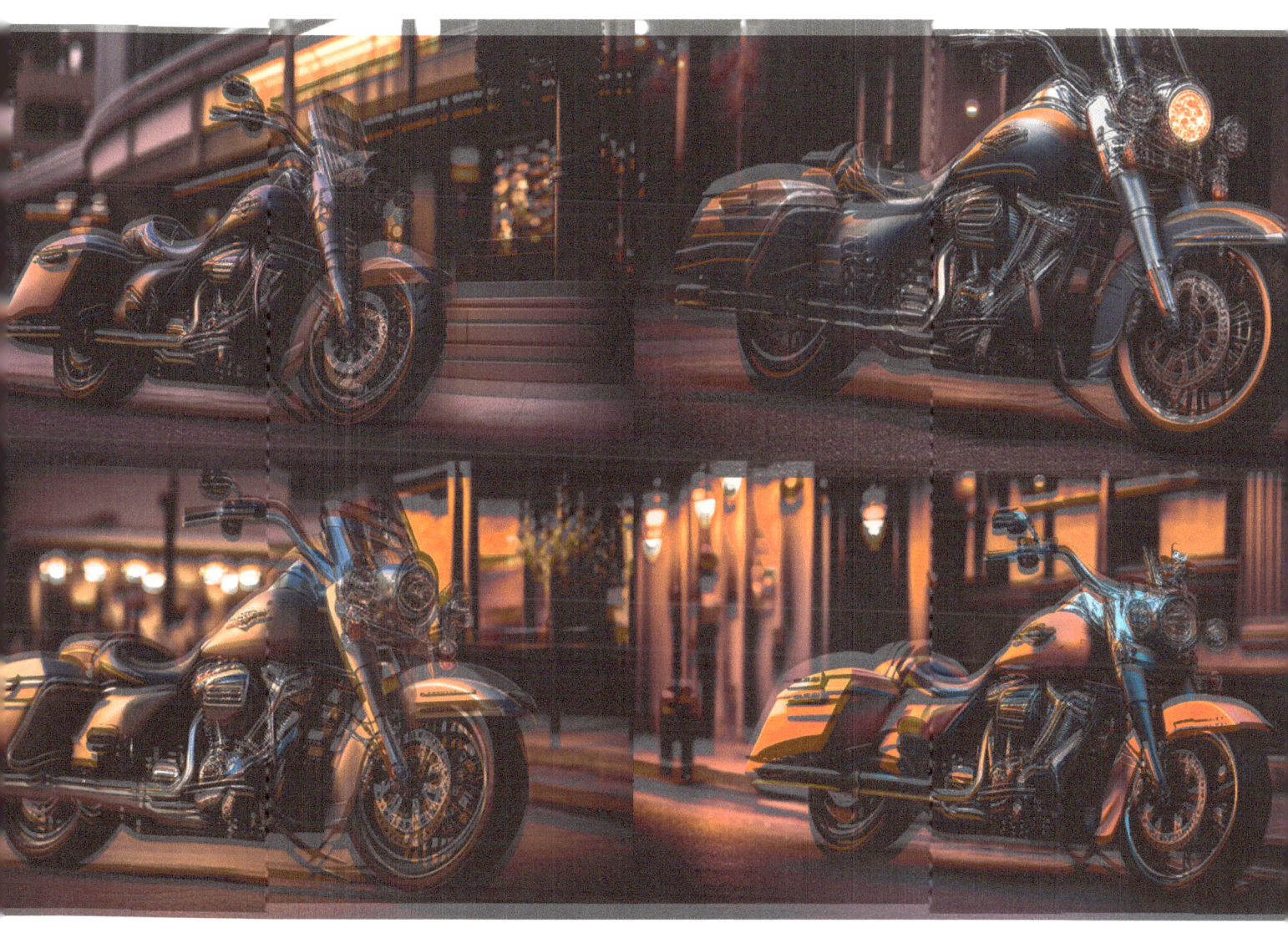

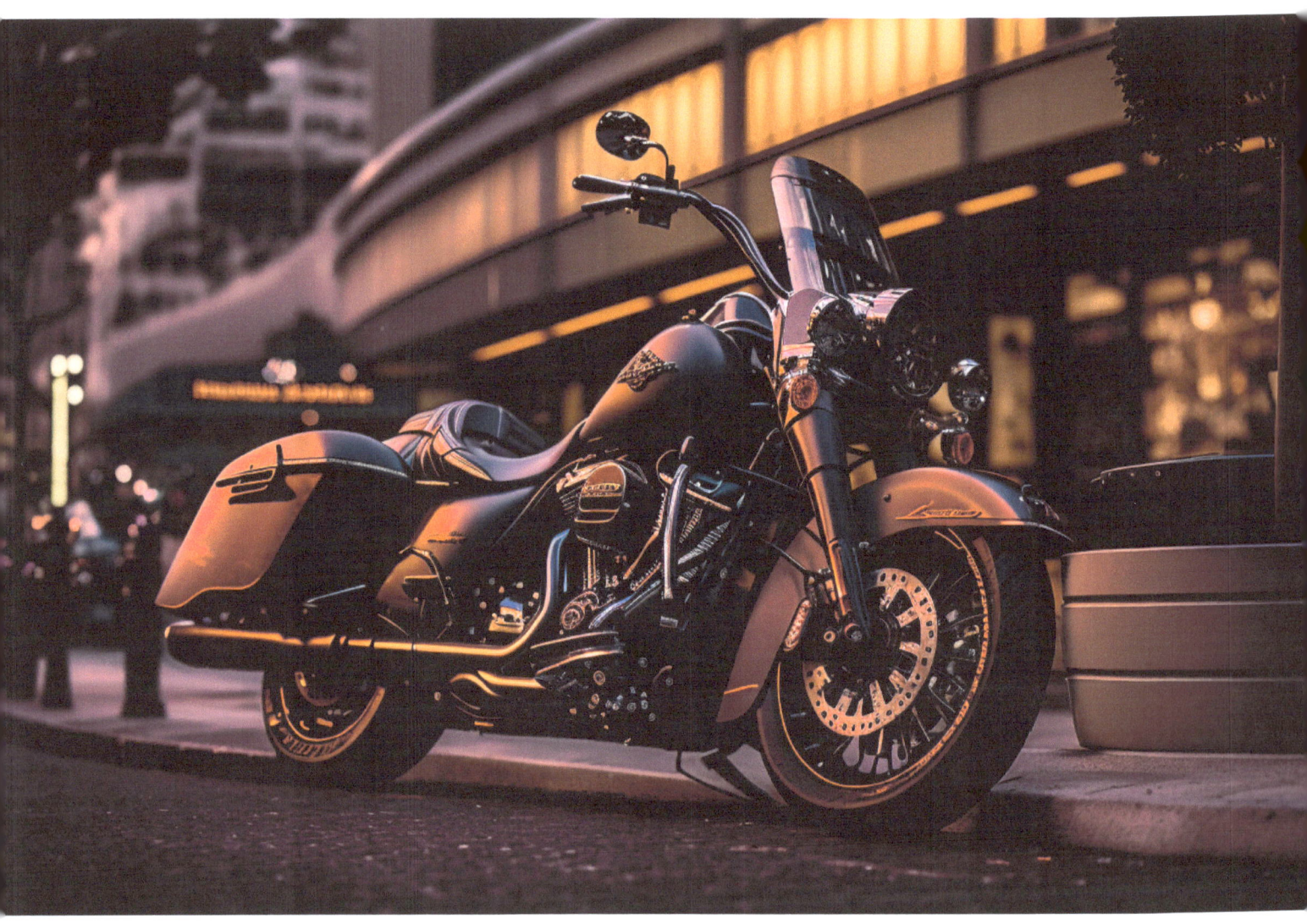

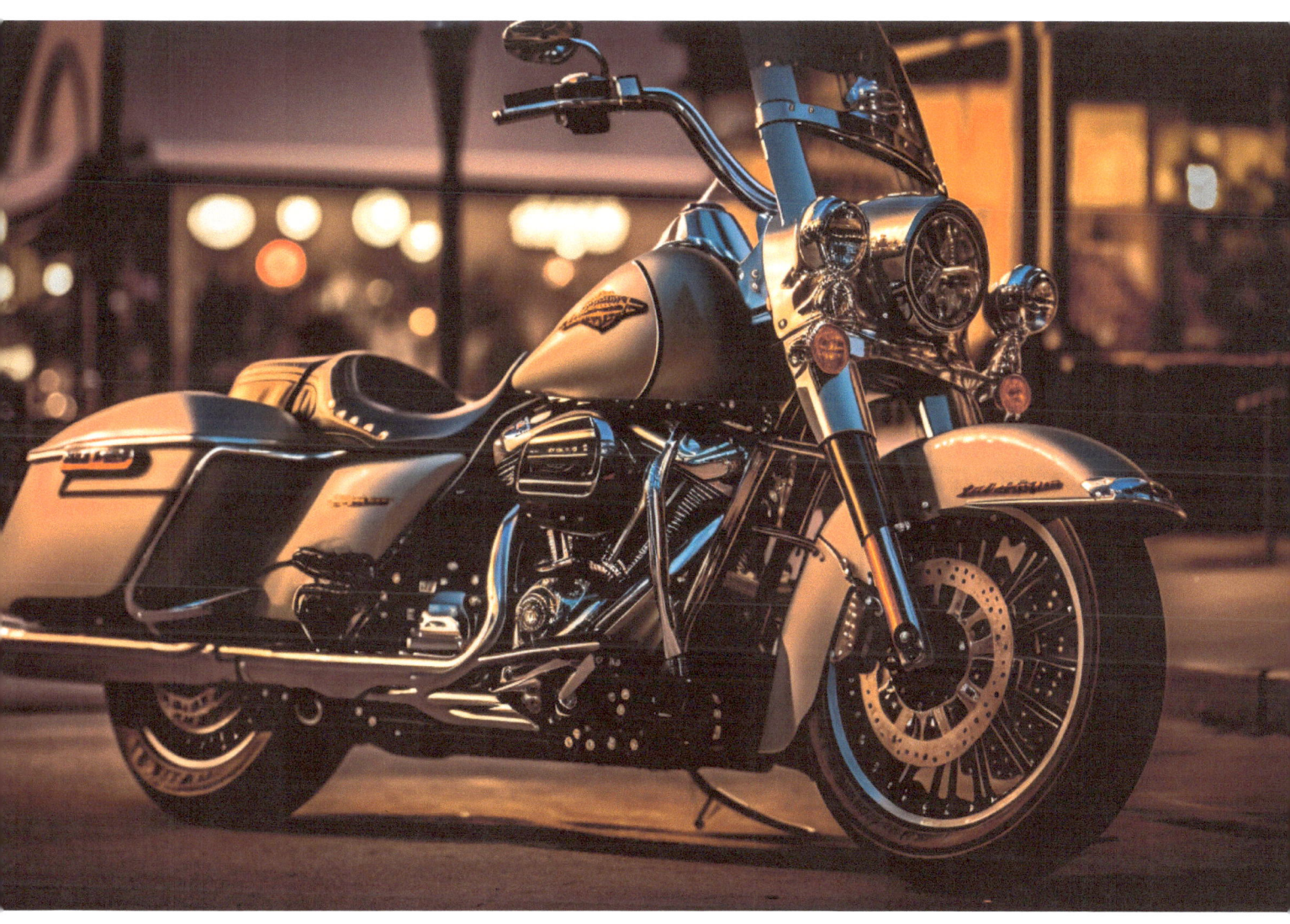

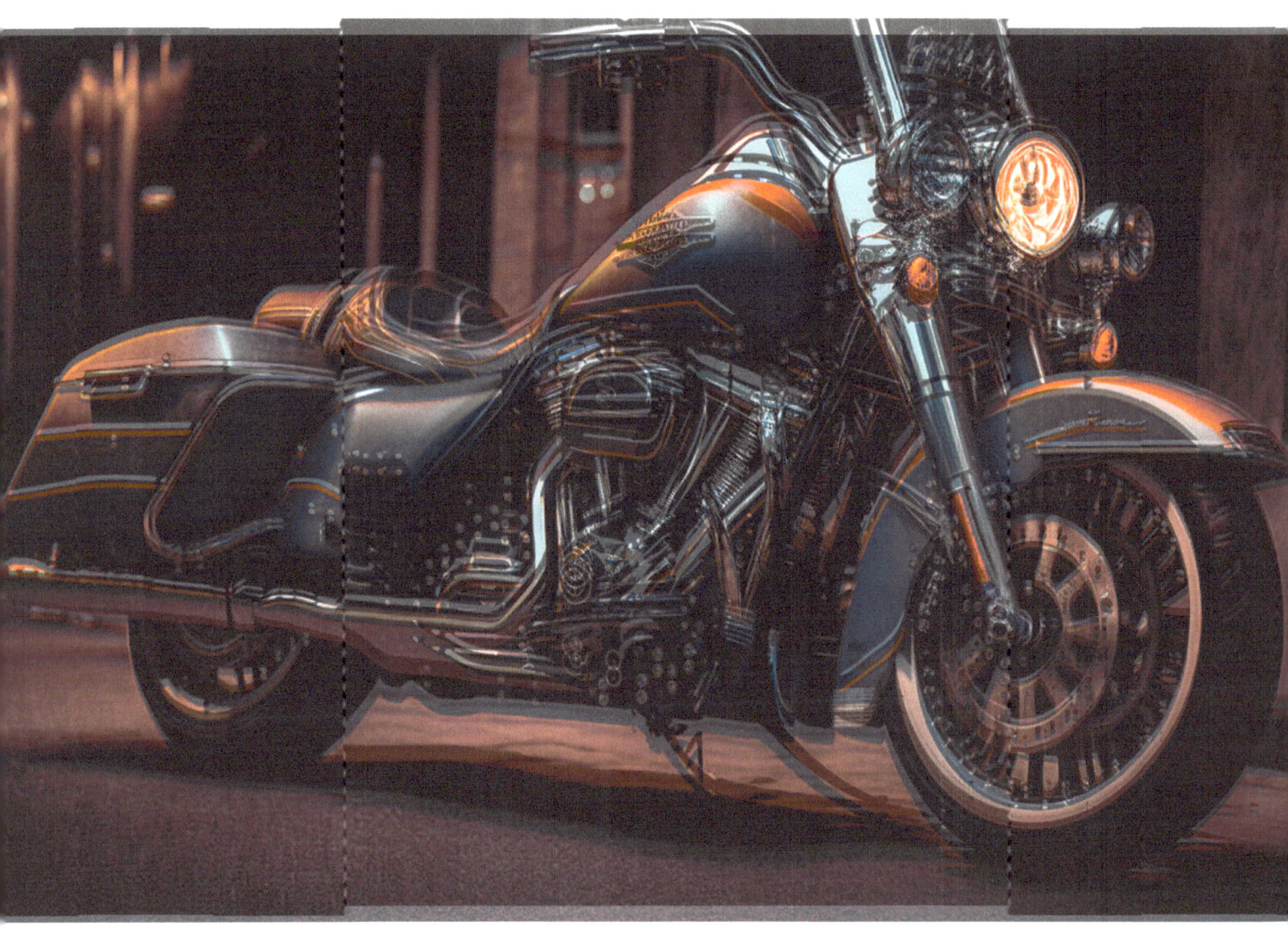

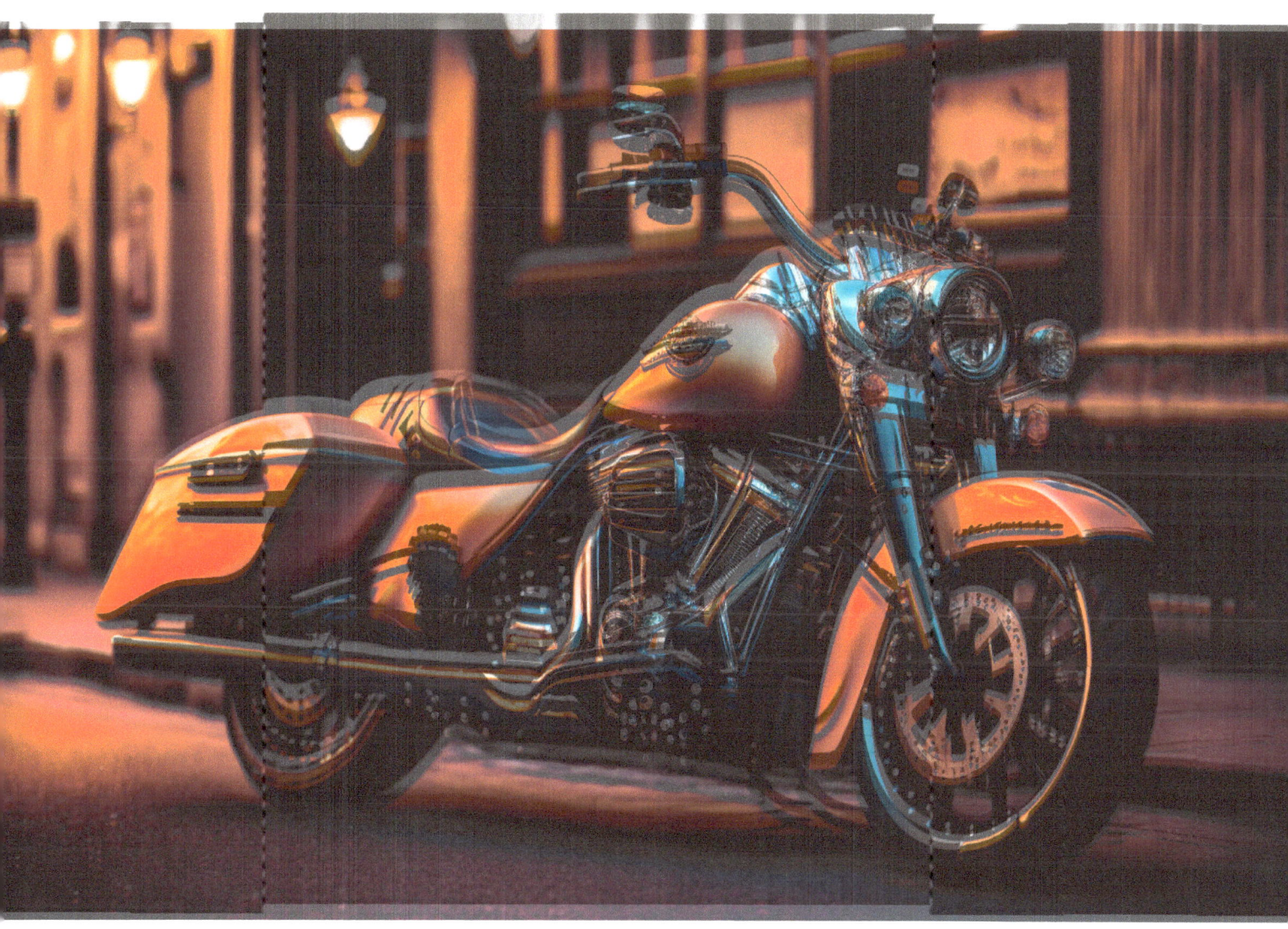

www.ingramcontent.com/pod-product-compliance
Lightning Source LLC
Chambersburg PA
CBHW051952210526
45473CB00023B/1737